"In the lineage of Mary Oliver and Wendell Berry, but with a resplendent eye and voice all her own, Heidi Barr's *Just Wild Enough* is a flowing meditation on the seasons that steps beyond the usual markers of the turning of the year. With a finely honed embodied attention, the poet guides us gracefully to places that hold an ever-present invitation to commune with the holy immanence of an enlivened Earth and the luminous insights that emerge when we do. C.G. Jung once said: 'People got dirty through too much civilization. Whenever we touch Nature, we get clean.' This is poetry that washes us clean."

—Frank Inzan Owen, author of *The School of Soft-Attention*

"Once again, Heidi Barr acts as guide to your inner and outer world. Exploring the directions and elements of each season, *Just Wild Enough* is a journey through the circle of a year, and a discovering of how to belong in this world. It asks, whether listening to bird songs, or hearing news of human injustice, are you wild enough to live life as a shared experience? You may lose yourself in the message of each poem. Yet, as in nature, it is in the quiet of this poetry where you remember what you really are."

—Esther Marcella Hoffman, author of *Love Note to Gaia*

"Reading *Just Wild Enough* puts us back into the flow of the seasons and reminds us of the restorative rhythm of life. Each verse holds the potential to enliven and reawaken us to the true nature of wildness. These words are written for the ones who love wild things as well as the ones who have been forgetting them."

—Catherine Brooks, Literary Apothecary, Curative Reading

"Barr speaks to us deeply as she follows the seasons and cardinal points in her new collection *Just Wild Enough* and the reader is enfolded into the light, sounds, and sensations of the natural world. Some poems feel as light and bright as morning dew, some roll in like a fog of presence, and some sing to the heart like wildflowers and birdsong. Such a gift invites us to slow down long enough to understand a life of wonder we might be missing and offers a celebration of what we can savor right now."

—Lisa Colón DeLay, author of *Wild Land Within* and host of *Spark My Muse* podcast

"*Just Wild Enough* conjures the best sort of longing in me—to walk in autumn woods or brew a cup of tea and watch the towhees from my favorite porch chair. Barr's poems are kind invitations into presence with the wildness waiting at our doorsteps and shimmering within us. She welcomes us into kinship with the natural world, coaxing us toward the gentle attentiveness required for living well."

—Krissy Kludt, poet and executive director of *Writing the Wild*

JUST

Wild

ENOUGH

New and Collected Poems

HEIDI BARR

WAYFARER BOOKS
BERKSHIRE MOUNTAINS, MASSACHUSETTS

WAYFARER BOOKS
WWW.WAYFARERBOOKS.ORG

© 2024 TEXT BY HEIDI BARR

All Rights Reserved
Published in 2024 by Wayfarer Books
Cover Design and Interior Design by Connor Wolfe
Cover Image © Barbara Brown
TRADE PAPERBACK 978-1-956368-82-6

10 9 8 7 6 5 4 3 2 1

Look for our titles in paperback, ebook, and audiobook wherever books are sold. Wholesale offerings for retailers available through Ingram.

Wayfarer Books is committed to ecological stewardship. We greatly value the natural environment and invest in conservation.

PO Box 1601, Northampton, MA 01060

860.574.5847 | info@homeboundpublications.com

HOMEBOUNDPUBLICATIONS.COM & WAYFARERBOOKS.ORG

For my daughter Eva

CONTENTS

SOUTH

WEST

NORTH

CENTER

Titles also by Heidi Barr

Nonfiction

Poetry

Most of the time I don't feel wild, not really—not like I imagine a wolf or river otter or loon must feel wild. Yet I do feel like at least a part of me is akin to rivers and lakes, soil and trees, and all the wild things that still crawl the earth, swim the seas, and soar the skies. That's the part I want to focus on. The part that's just wild enough. Attention to that part is a prayer, the kind that rises from the ordinary, the kind that harmonizes with all the other wild parts of creation in a collective song of everyday devotion, a song that persists through all seasons, across all borders, and rides on the winds of time.

Elemental

I knew someone once
who was air rising
ethereal energy, atmosphere embodied.

I knew someone once
who was flame dancing—
a burst of fire and smoke reaching skyward.

I knew someone once
who was water seeping—
a pervasive holy presence finding a way.

I knew someone once
who was earth standing—
solid rock channeling unwavering truth.

It was you, or me, maybe all of us
—air, fire, water, earth—
meeting in space and across time

a collective effervescence
a collision of earth and sky
a confluence of all that once was and yet will be.

EAST

To the winds of the East—may you bless us with your call
toward spring, your freshness of being, your breeze that offers
clear vision and new perspective. May we look toward the
winged ones—egret, butterfly, eagle—aloft with ease, gentle,
honoring our younger selves, evolving as life calls us to evolve,
always remembering that fierce newness is with us in every step.

The young ones

Through the tree cover
or prairie grasses waving
in the fading light
of a day fully lived,

they squeal in jubilation
over a thumb-sized toad
a bucket of soil
a crimson raspberry

always embodying
an evolving understanding
what it means to be alive
and present in this place,

seeping into earth's
ever-present breath
through the moments
that make up a life

spent in the shade
of the brightness
in the shadow
made by the sun

and all the other things
that come
when someone new decides
to be on earth.

That was then

This is now. And when you can remember
that you are made of the same stuff as stars—
the same stuff as the blossom
turning its face to the morning sun,
the breeze that carries your hope for you
when you forget to pick it up in the morning—
you can sense something extraordinary
in the simple act of getting back up,
in remembering to breathe, in remembering
you are always connected to the mystery
that makes you human, even when
you have to scrape off the grime
to let your radiance pierce the darkness.

How to go home again

Put down technology, just for a while.
Pick up any aspect of your identity
that has gotten lost over the years
and remember what it feels like
to hold it close, unfiltered.
Step outside and stride
to the center of the nearest woodland.
Lay down under the still-bare canopy,
heart open to the sky, hearing
with your whole body
how sun and rain and soil
thaw the frozen bits of you,
reminding you to fully melt
into your place in the wild
family of things.

Acquiescence

Some years
spring arrives
in a release of warm air,
mud seeping around boots
as the frost lets go until next time.

But more often
spring arrives
holding on tight to winter's chill
snow crunching underfoot, everyone
wishing for warmth that isn't quite here.

No matter how
spring arrives
on that vernal equinox
light and dark are balanced—
poised to usher in something new,
or reclaim something very very old
something that pushes through
cold soil, intent on emerging
when the time is right.

Collisions of lake and lawn

The lake is higher
than it's ever been—

from the deck I can see
wood ducks swimming

across part of the lawn,
where water laps a new spot of shore.

They paddle through brown reeds
as icy wind pushes me back inside.

A fire is going, despite the late spring day,
and I'm thinking about unanswerable questions

as this poem I'm writing doesn't, maybe, want
to be a poem—it wants to be words stretched out across the page
with no profound lesson or tidy lines bound together by a witty
title or effective line breaks that convey a meaning maybe not
even the writer of the lines can uncover. It wants to be more like
high water in a cold spring, going where its momentum takes it,
swimming furiously across unruly waters, reaching until there's
nowhere left to go and it's time to recede

back into tidy lines
looking for the lessons
in how a wood duck swims
in a yard swallowed
by the season.

Things I wanted to photograph but didn't

How soil feels after three seasons away
New bursts of air on skin bared to the breeze
Otters making their way across the ripples of the lake
Rain's anticipatory scent hanging low over the landscape
An apple blossom's first blush, slowly opening to the season
Cacophonies of bird and frog song, a wild symphony of sound
Pea shoots and rhubarb rushes, garlic growth and daisies dancing
Spring's fusion of muted palettes and the burst of fuchsia flowers
Gardens gradually growing into their own, and then suddenly,
                                        life everywhere.
How contentment can sneak up on a person
who takes the time to omit that which doesn't give life, instead
focusing on those things that bring peace and stretch time
into something to savor, letting what is be simply whole
even when it's undocumented, only experienced
as another layer of texture in a life fully lived,
a life full of photographs not taken
because some things are meant
to be threads weaving
light uncaptured.

Everyday enchantment

Look for the magic
that falls from the sky
or tumbles from tree tops
enchanting a bit of earth
for a little while — then
you can return
to business as usual
if you like — or
you could let that magic
meld with your own,
a reminder that it's always
there when you need it.

Rainy days in spring

Rainy days in spring
are for walking quietly
through gently falling water
are for well-thumbed books
read in early afternoon
are for tea steeping
while drops drum the roof
are for land and sky
working together
through mess and necessity
to keep the world turning
ice and mud eventually coming
to an agreement that's green
with potential for growing
with potential for blooming
with potential for feeding
weary souls wandering
on rainy days in spring.

Hover

Sometimes single
moments hold still
in a way that allows
knowing just what
it feels like to be
where you are.

Cheers

to sunshine
that drags its feet
but gets here eventually

to warmth
that finds soil
and welcomes seeds, finally

to spring days
that reflect hope
in what could yet be

to spring evenings
that remind you
to be here now.

Breathe a river of light

You are breath's shadow and a river
of light, a remnant of stars and moon
dancing, an expression of bliss housed
in a body, a confluence of cells that will
never come together in the same way again,
one thread in the great web that connects all things
raindrops and pipestone, a dream with memory,
something perfection can't touch because
perfection doesn't exist when you are
a joyfully made, messily gorgeous thing.

A sign of good medicine

Even when
it's cold and raining
you don't miss
a dose.

—on going outside

Joy will come

It's that time of year,
a collective uncurling
days lengthening, sun strengthening—

spring imminent on the horizon.

It seems all the world
is ready to rejoice,
lamenting a long winter.

(Are we talking about the weather?)

Cold and ice have their place
in the story of the world,
even now, even if rejoicing

seems hard to come by.

Joy will come, it's time is near
especially when winter
is not something to fear.

Winter and spring together are magic.

Maple sap only runs
when warm days keep
company with frozen nights.

Harbinger

The wind was blowing,
cold, out of the north
as a hawk cried
then circled, high above
clouds billowing and gray.

60 miles south, Minneapolis:
grief and outrage build—
a tiny boy suddenly and violently
without a dad while a man who's already dead
stands trial for his own murder[1].

Snow will fall
this Easter season.
It's expected.
It will still startle us.
Can it startle us enough?

---

[1] During former Minneapolis police officer Derick Chauvin's trial for the killing of
George Floyd, lines of questioning by the defense often brought Mr. Floyd's charac-
ter into question. During the trial, Daunte Wright, a Black father of a small boy, was
shot and killed by Minnesota police officers.

Studies in resurrection

Then, suddenly, a new kind
of hope appears, the kind that
walks the earth bathed in light
because it already survived fire,
a holy risen thing that steps
from ashes to companion
whatever comes next.

SOUTH

To the winds of the south—as you usher in summer, may we
accept your invitation to step into a time of blossoming, of
warmth—a season ripe with reminders of our inner flame. May
we tend our passionate, confident, relational selves, honoring
transformation, healing, and the power of love.

Go back, 1

Take me back
to that place
under a quiet sky
where dragonfly wings
make joyful music, fish dance
beneath intertwining lily pads,
moss stretches out
in welcome underfoot.
Remind me to pause
just long enough
to be swept up
by the magic
of the kingdom.

Passion

Sometimes flowers
look more like flames
reminding us that we, too,
can disrupt the usual
with unexpected fire.

Just wild enough

I wander toward stillness
as fog rolls into the valley,

cranes crooning overhead,
wildflowers swaying, sun

swiftly sinking in the westerly sky
nudging me to notice

what needs remembering
to step toward the next moment

fully human and wild enough
to be find solace in silence,

a wild silence that coats the land
with goodness and grace

which is, as Wendell Berry might say,
the peace of wild things.

Directions to a more beautiful world

Imagine a bridge
between water and sky
then take one step
after another
until you meet
justice and restoration
keeping company
with love and belonging.
Then keep walking
toward peace.

Wild sweet

Find your time
open to what is
step toward what will be while
understanding your place is here
—where you are—
yet also where you will be
—or could be—
        someday.

Depending on your perspective

It's a day
for celebration
& joy
a day
for wealth redistribution
& reparations
a day
to remember
& grieve
a day
to listen
& honor
shared histories
colliding
to move together
into right action,
where love is a verb
that hears, helps,
& heals a way
forward

—on Juneteenth as a federal holiday
—on Indigenous Peoples Day

Illumination

That day the sun came out
to talk to the moon
and all the beauty of earth agreed
that essential things—
reclamations of rightness
calls for community
celebrations of cultural contribution
transformations that allow full embodiment—
are necessary to recognize;
are reasons to rejoice.

—on Transgender day of visibility

Possibilities

Lilies blooming
remind me how
water, earth, and sun
still conspire,
making beauty possible
despite everything.

How to become poetry

Find the verse in birds singing
in fallen feathers
in rustles of old leaves
in ripples that caress calm waters
in softness that stretches out inside summer heat.
Allow it to fill you up,
skin absorbing every line,
a reminder that you are song walking—
old leaves rustling
calm waters rippling,
a softness that hovers
coaxing attentiveness into art.

A recipe for one kind of pleasure

First decide to be here
and just here, but leave a little room
for memory and hopeful expectation.
Then, slice a zucchini, maybe some garlic,
to just the size you like it. Chop fresh basil
into ribbons of scent, and slip
a serrated knife through a fleshy
orange tomato, one just off the vine,
because that's your favorite kind
and it's ripe and ready to taste.
Let the juice go where it will
as you drop it all into sizzling oil
hot enough to alchemize
such delight into nourishment.
Let the reminder of high summer
and the anticipation of right now
carry you into the ecstasy
of harmonizing with yourself.

Conversations

Practice being
still enough
for conversations
with wildflowers.

We are one body

Sometimes sky and water
forget who's who
and the world remembers
what it's like to be one body.

Why I walk in the woods

To remember
  to be alive
    with my whole self.

Instructions for living

Stand quietly
and let wisdom
come to you.

Sungold

There are too many
of you to pick
all at once—
after all, we're just one small family—
though I try to keep up with your abundance,
your sweetness dropping
into my hands, onto the soil, bursting between my teeth,
a taste of summer
that I never used to like but do now.
Now I crave you when you aren't here
and that makes me glad your season is short—
abundance is sweetest when bookended by desire.

In solitude or when keeping company

Do not underestimate
the power of good music,
beautiful food, and a pace
that allows remembering
how to savor,
delicate notes trading harmonies
with a brave voice, or
simple flavors mingling
on your tongue—
a ordinary sacred joining
of taste and presence.

Wildness

There isn't enough time
between what I've just done
and what is coming next, but
I pull into the gravel lot anyway.

I park the car and walk through a corridor
of towering pines. The wind is murmuring
as I pick my way down a rocky ravine
and slip off a sun-warmed rock into cold rushing water.

Wildness swallows
the too-full day
and leaves the here and now
in its place.

Trees across the river

Through smoke-hazy air
across the river fly birds

underbellies flashing bright white
against impossible green.

Water flows low at the hands of drought,
dryness leaving the shore parched and brittle

where softness once was.
Farm irrigation and garden hoses stretch

for miles as black snakes
feed on ancient light.

Even the moss on the trees feels the effects
of the times, crying out for rain,

hoping beyond hope
that something will change

that no more black snakes
are born and fed with oil

that more people will remember
water is life

that more people will act
in ways that keep

that ancient light
in the ground.

Dragonfly

One day you rise up,
great clouds of you everywhere—
suddenly present after months of absence.
You are beautiful in your transparency
and your persistence. You are delicate,
yet nimble. You can be still and calm,
yet move with speed and intent
when necessary. You remind me
what humans are capable of
when we rise up together
in what matters.

Sometimes love

Is holding space
Is right in front of you
Is bridging the gap
Is accepting imperfection
Is walking alone in a woodland
Is being carried on a rough road
Is carrying someone else
Is saying the right goodbye
Is waiting long enough
Is telling the truth
Is screaming in righteous rage
Is listening with open eyes
Is weeping with open hearts
Is diving into bliss
Is everything

Worth repeating

Disappear into something
wonderfully and beautifully made—
the possibility of dawn
the brilliance of midday sun
the surrender of late afternoon
the glow of golden hour
the gentle noise of night.
Get lost in the moments
and emerge more beautiful,
more wonder-filled
than before.

Details of small things

I made a pact with a jumping spider
just the other day when he was waiting
for whatever jumping spiders wait for
as they traverse sides of municipal trash bins.
After that, a lichen-studded log engaged me in conversation
about slow living, allowing ample space
for listening to lonesome leaves
discern their response as they littered
about in our invitation to join.
You just never know what might take root
when you peer deeply into the details of small things,
mind open to alternative ways of communication,
all the while acknowledging despite everything,
that pact has love for the world at its center.

Precipice

Cold will come one of these days.
But not yet.

Today summer is holding on to its glory,
breeze warm enough to invite open windows

and a stationary perch on a dock.
Under the water's surface,

plants are breaking down, readying
themselves for stillness and decay.

But on top the lily pads flaunt
full blooms, as if they are telling me

that though a shift is coming,
it's not time to wish for it.

It's time to savor the season that is.

Perseverance

Living each day
is a valiant act of hope
a walk through courage
an embodiment of bold
love for self and the world;
every breath, no matter
how hard to draw and
each step, no matter
how hard to take
singular works of art
essential to the creation
of miracles.

WEST

To the winds of the west, a turning toward autumn—may we
see your illustration of how to experience fluidity as we step
into a deepening understanding of ourselves and an evolving
appreciation for all that is. As you hold your mirror to our faces,
we know you will not look away. May we sink with gratitude
into your depths and emerge cleansed, awake,
and fortified for what's still to come.

Commune

Go to where
water walks by the sky
springs live in deep pools
and rainbows dance toward night.
Emerge cleansed and ready
for whatever comes next.

I'll fly away

Time between seasons
stands still and flies away,
lily studded water
holding light on the surface
as clouds gather in witness
offering reason to be right here
walking the edge of transition.

Go back, 2

Go back
to that place
under a quiet sky
where sandhill cranes
trill an ancient song
where leaves dance
on their way to decay,
where frost closes one
door to open another.
Remember to pause
just long enough
to be enchanted
by the magic
of the kingdom.

Spectrum

Emerson said
the earth laughs
in flowers and while
I think that's true,
I think the earth
also grieves and rages
sings and remembers
a full spectrum of feeling
along with the joy
of her bloom
through rooting and reaching
budding and blossoming
letting tired petals
fall to the ground
or float away on a breeze
when the season
of growth is done.

Celestial reminders

Approach this equinox
poised to jump over flames,
balance making ready for the march
toward gathering dark.
Embrace the fire in your heart,
a fire that always stays lit, burning
what you no longer need to ash
dispersed in moonbound smoke,
smoke that tames any dragons
that wait in the slanting shadows
of deepening night, fearsome
beasts becoming fluid beauty.
      —on Michaelmas

Stranger

I wonder sometimes
if we were brothers
in another life
or doctor and patient, maybe even lovers
you caring for me, or me for you
us for each other
lives intimately intertwined
as time stretches out
in a trajectory
we'll never know, at least
not in this life.
And I ask myself
if wondering about that other life
could be enough
to heal the wounds
of this one.

Aid stations everywhere

Be an aid station
not to put yourself last
and care for everyone else
but to create a life raft—
a love big enough to carry
replenishment for the tired
medicine and healing for the sick
nourishment for the hungry
a simple vessel of clean water
      for those who thirst.
Let your life lift the lives of others
because when we all do it
aid stations are everywhere.

Here for it

Apple trees dripping with fruit
branches heavy with sweet nourishment

Gourds and squashes laying exposed
vines snaking over spent fields

Fog rising from the valley at dawn
water and air forming clouds of misty light

Golden crunchy carpets of leaves
blanketing the ground with a new layer of depth

Tractors and trucks, combines and semis
racing against the clock of harvest time

Wood cracking under the ax
logs stacked high in piles of reassurance

Winds that strip maples of brightness
leaving living skeletons in their wake

Letting the season settle so deep in your bones
that when it's time, you're ready to let it go.

Dear apple

In the early years
I served you mashed
with a fork, or whirled
in the blender
tiny bites taken
hesitantly, then heartily;
baby's first fruit.

After awhile you were chopped
into little bits, equal parts
food and plaything
juicy and gleefully
flung across the table
and onto the floor.

Then, you were most desirable
peeled, sliced finely
into uniform half-moons
always eaten
as one last requirement.

Today you are sliced
packed into a lunch bag
or chomped right off the tree—
something to look forward to
when leaves turn crimson &
caramel is its own food group.

Thank you for being
a growing up companion,
so malleable
so nourishing
so consistently here
year after year.

Courage

Look close enough
to notice the purple flowers
that insist on persisting
even when it might
be easier to give in
and fade;
even if every other year
until now they've laid down
their petals in silence.
But for this one, and that one, and her too,
the time for speaking up is today
as a new kind of power
a collective rage, channeled
into right action coats the land
with the sort of courage
shared with purple flowers, the ones
who bloom in the season of autumn,
return with a fierce beauty,
reminding us that truth
always finds a way
to speak and be heard.

Discernment

Here is the Amanita mushroom,
red with dainty white spots,
straight out of a storybook—
pretty and poisonous
discovered just now
while wandering
from house to garden,
not food for us but perhaps
home to a fairy or two,
the kind who know their way
around beautiful lethal things.

A miracle of sound and soul

It happens when
you allow yourself to be held—
undercurrents of necessary energy
your foundation, along with knowledge
that you come from generations of survival.

It happens when
breath and movement
coalesce into kriyas,
awareness and expansion
rising up your spine like a wave.

It happens when
a tsunami of sound builds,
funneling life-force toward
a collective release
a shedding of the old

as roots tunnel deeper
into the truth that can carry you
down a healing river,
the river that's always there
when you allow yourself

to be held by the confluence
of sound and soul.

On grief

It takes as long as it takes.

There is no right way to do it,
no stages you must achieve
to move to the next, no timeline
that must be followed for optimal recovery.

You don't have a disorder.
You don't have to find a silver lining
or get over anything.

You don't have to use your loss
as a way to achieve enlightenment
or progress to another level of personal development.

Explore telling the truth, even if it's hard
for others to hear it. Explore what existing
inside loss looks like, what it means
to absorb it into your being, what it means
to tend to your pain.

(If the grief isn't yours,
explore sitting in the discomfort of allowing
another their own experience without trying to fix it.)

This takes as long as it takes.

Breath by breath you figure out
how to carry it, and maybe a sharp edge
or two softens after a while. Maybe not.

(There is no right way to do it.)

However you tend, move through
instead of over, the wildest part of love
a companion on the way.

Brilliant with dying

Today started
in a wash of gold,
tangerine and burnt umber

competing or complimenting
—I'm never certain which—
reminders to be astonished.

I hope they know
their peak is witnessed
appreciated and celebrated

brilliant in decline
brilliant even
because of it.

As the great wheel turns

It's a time to celebrate
harvest, but also
those who have gone before,
as marching
toward darkness
reminds us how shadows
and their spirits
offer a sense of wholeness
to the wheel of the year.
>   —on Samhain
>   —on All Saints Day

If you believe the sky

November is when things happen—
It's a time, or maybe a place within time
where silence stretches out
to absorb the sandhill crane's song
where clouds seem to drop toward the water
to meet the splash of a beaver's tail
where the gardener of time pauses,
reaching for the reflection of stillness.
A November sky is a nudge to see beauty
in that which fades, in that which persists,
in seeds that float away in the cold wind,
in creatures who make ready for winter,
in the energy that exists between dreams and waking
and memory that wanders through mist.

On certainty

What do you know for sure?
Even if it isn't much, there's something—
what you're standing on, the way the leaves dancing
through fading light make you feel,
the shirt you always feel good wearing,
which foods remind you
of home, who you love, maybe
even who loves you—keep it close,
lean on it when not knowing
tries to push you down.
What do you know for sure?

On uncertainty

There's always something unknown
hovering, sitting on your shoulder
chirping questions,
a tiny thorny orb of wondering,
a second skin that never quite settles
a chord that isn't in complete alignment
because it's still being created
and that's the allure of it, thorns and all—
moments keep unfolding, and somehow
rough edges and deep, dark grooves
along with enough softness to cradle chaos,
provide the foundation
for a life in progress, allowing
what comes next to be a beautifully
destructive invitation to dance.

Necessary undoing

after Krissy Kludt

Darkness, be an undoing.
Unravel threads that try too hard,
holding tight to brightness
where shadow is better suited
for stitching a path through the unknown.

Darkness, be an undoing.
Drape a cloak of velvety black
over the threshold between wrong
and right, allowing enough time
in liminal space to feel a way forward.

Darkness, be an undoing.
Welcome tentative steps
taken in faith through uncertainty
each one an act of courage
an undoing necessary to be whole.

NORTH

To the winds of the north, Mother Earth—may we welcome
your energy and your power as winter's stillness spreads
across the land—an energy that brings clarity, boundaries, and
precision. May your gift of stillness give us strength to cut away
what is no longer needed. To say yes and no when each is called
for. To rise into what stillness can offer.

Go back, 3

Go back
to that place
—the wild silence within—
where peace is a river
running through your veins
where tall buildings
are an invitation to look up,
where inner quiet is more
powerful than outer chaos.
Remember to pause
just long enough
to be swept up
into the miracle
of mindfulness.

No small thing

It is no small thing

to forgive yourself

to accept what is

to begin again

to feel like enough.

The spirituality of stillness

What if silence
is much more than
the absence of noise

is a rooting down
is a looking way up
is a quality of being

that isn't free of sound
but rather a space to exist
more fully grounded

in the possibility of who
you truly are, a way to witness
your full self being born?

No-man's-land

This is the place,
the land of being too busy
yet somehow under-stimulated
and exceedingly worried
that the busyness will vanish,
this busyness that you feel
you should be exceedingly grateful to have.

And you are, truly—
on one hand it's a sort of privilege
to be busy and maybe even get paid for it.
Or to be busy and feel needed.

Maybe you're busy
and it feels like the world requires you
to keep being busy no matter what.

Maybe you stay busy because when you stop
it's hard to know who you are.

And that's the scary thing, isn't it?

Yet when the gears grind to a halt
there's silence filling the empty space
where busyness used to be—
and that empty space might be
more hospitable than you think.

Space

The weary world
wants nothing more
than to rejoice

claim victory
reunite with what's gone
missing.

It's tempting,
that pull to fill the void
as quickly as possible—

after a fallow season,
during deep winter
when hunger seems

it might eat you alive
in your wanting.
Those times can feel bleak.

What happens
when you let what feels empty
settle over you

like a cloud—
impermanent, with
a promise of possibility?

The art of idling

Sit still. Stand. Lay down. Whatever suits you.
Tap a foot or bounce a knee if necessary.
Sink at your own pace into the space
cleared by not doing.
Resist the urge to _____.
(discern urgent from distraction)
Notice resistance, any craving
to engage with something other than
your own thoughts and sensations.
Let boredom be there until
it loses interest in you and dissolves—
joining its energy with the quality of being
that allows you to find life
deep within the void.

On omitting

They say you can learn to love
the sound of your footsteps walking
away from that not meant for you, and
I think that's true, even though at first
the sound is a jarring dissonance humming
at the edges of your skin, until you realize
the humming turns harmonious
when your skin is wrapped
around only what's yours.

Unexpected places

As the longest night
approaches, inviting us
into a new season, the muskrat
I saw swimming earlier today, so alive
beneath clear ice four inches thick,
is a reminder to recognize that life
can spring forth, swimming furiously,
from the most unexpected places.

Winter solstice—shortest day, longest night—

in a stretch of years defined by "unprecedented" could be pretty bleak. Light and dark are as far from balanced as it gets. Planets align in once in a lifetime ways, the moon is eclipsed by blood. Much of the globe is shrouded in darkness, literally and figuratively, sometimes both. It's cold at my house, and the wind is hissing through the woodlands that are still devoid of the snow we welcome this time of year. I look up and see mostly clouds. But my candle still flickers against an inky black sky, and the wind, if I listen closely, doesn't hiss. It hums an ancient rhythm that is woven deeper than anything unprecedented ever could.

—in the year 2020 &

—in years yet to come

In deep winter

I like a quiet evening

at home

close to a fire

listening to the wind

soft music

the way a body

shifts to find comfort.

Fallow time it may be,

peace dwells

in the empty space

in ideas yet to come

in each wispy tendril

floating skyward—

smoke signals

of ordinary grace.

Hoarfrost morning

Waking up
to a frosted prairie,
each ice crystal
a hushed moment
of rapture.

What hope has to say

Can little bits of hope
fill in the cracks of last year,
or the ones that came before?
It's not my place to say, not
really. I can say I see hope
on the horizon clear as day
but that doesn't make it true
for anyone else.

That doesn't mean it's not true either.

What does hope look like
for you, today, right now?
Can you see it in your mind's eye?
What would it feel like if you could
hold it in your hands? What would
it be like if it could hold you?

What would hope say to you
if you listened with whatever senses
were available?

Maybe little bits of hope do
fill in the cracks of years gone by:

By way of a child's innocent glee
By way of a man set free to go
By way of a woman telling the truth
By way of gender not defining a person
By way of all love celebrated

All bodies cherished
All colors seen
All waters protected
All spectrums essential

All ways of being
different ways of experiencing
the path that leads us back to each other.

Star child

Be absorbed

by a new moon
slicing a night sky

by river ice
cracking in creation

by skeletal trees
cloaked in frost

by cold air
directing attention

by a million stars
calling you by a name you used to know

one that was part of you
before you were born.

Be absorbed
by what you already are.

Moonbound

Some nights cold
polishes the moon to a sliver ,
a luminescent slice of light
hanging in the western sky.

Ice fully claims the lake,
waters stilled by gusty winds
into frozen waves
that will be cresting til thaw.

Hearth flames dance and crackle,
burning away any chills threatening
to cling, sending them skyward
on tendrils of moon-bound smoke.

Untitled

You could make this place beautiful[2]
is a line spoken by many, but it's also
a line true for anyone willing
to look past the rough edges
or peer into darkness through a soft lens,
anyone tending a wound
bound in shadow or with cuts
on their way to healing
but that aren't quite there,
anyone who holds room for possibility
on a lonely lingering day in a winter
intent on holding on tight—
even then, you could make this place beautiful.

---

[2] A few examples of those who have said that line are Maggie Smith, whose book of that title came out in April 2023, and many a realtor showing a house for sale.

No small thing, 2

It is no small thing
to wake up in a warring world,
unconditional positive regard
bleeding out at your feet
empathy cleaved into ribbons
by the gods of vengeance, to
notice, even on the darkest of
dawns, a small bird singing
songs that rise up anyway—
tiny offerings that may not heal
the open wound but add
just enough light to keep you
working toward peace.

Collective rising

Let your wings unfold,
an emergence of grace and power,
courage rising with each breath
as you uncover the best balance
of give and take, simple acts
of discernment filling you up
with the kind of energy
that ensures the only limits
you encounter are those
of your own making, set there
to encourage the replenishment
necessary to rise stronger still,
ready to acknowledge your worth
and soar into the sort of stillness
that serves your life best.

CENTER

To the center, the swirling mystery that is the source of all things,
a source that goes by many names and is of all origins,
colors, and creeds—we honor the unknown that pervades
all of life, and we hold space for all that you contain.
We remember that every breath can hold a prayer
when we allow ourselves to touch the core.

Life on earth

We—you and I; them and us—
we're like a great web,

spider silk stretching out
beyond horizons

Aspen roots intertwined
binding us together

clouds of misty fog
permeating our cells over here

and theirs over there.
In some ways we live apart, yet

we remain connected
through space and across time

all generations and species
colors and creeds

different parts yet one body
of blood and bone, soil and sky.

Thin places

I was thinking today
about words that come alive
on your tongue, an embodied host;
about beauty that evaporates
when touched, so keep reaching;
about seekers reading poetry,
finding prayer in the lines—
about breath air life art
jumbled up vibrations,
humanity meeting itself
in the space between.

Despite everything

When despair for the world
grows, creeping its way in,
sending shoots of anxiety snaking
everywhere, turn to where
flowers grow instead, insistent
on brilliantly blooming bright,
bursts of sunlight shining
expectant faces turned toward sky,
them tending you
while you tend them.
Take what is heavy
from your shoulders
and rest for a time
in the beauty
that remains.

Let your attention be a prayer

Today
and all days

let your attention
be a prayer
rolling with fog
over still waters.

Let your attention
be a prayer
absorbing warm sun,
an ingestion of light.

Let your attention
be a prayer
joining birds and frogs
in making a joyful noise.

Let your attention
be a prayer
one that fuses
with all other prayers

rising in a great cloud
of collected healing—
Earth's congregation
connected in community

attention to the wild
the gateway to devotion.

Oneness

We could say
you are God, and
so am I, along with
that barn owl and the field
of yellow flowers and those two
crows, the ones sitting atop a
huge blue spruce, peering
down, seeming to know
much more than I do
about the ways of
the universe.

Sensing divinity

See—
Sacred revealed
in unexpected ways.

Hear—
The fight for justice
keeping company with songs of peace.

Feel—
Love tracing your jaw
with the slightest breeze.

Taste—
Plant, sun, water coursing through veins,
ingestions of holy alchemy.

Holy golden things

Wander where the trees
reach high in witness
where big bluestem
bows down in prayer
where wild aster
looks you in the eye
where fallen leaves
crunch in welcome.
See how goldenrod
readies itself for the turn
when the world becomes
a holy golden thing.

Remembrance

The fallen leaf
has a song in it
one that sings
like a prayer,
a surrender
to a season
that fades
into another life
where ghosts walk,
heads held high,
an acknowledgement
of what was
keeping company
with what could yet be,
a holy wildness
right there underfoot.

Collective rising, 2

It's there in the witness
pain held with softness
struggle not stopped, but seen
a momentary link, a fusion
made by acknowledging scars
and not fearing the open wound
a connection that slows any bleeding
just enough to let the feathers
of other birds hold the line,
tiny fierce cradles of love,
wisps of active hope, rising.

Metamorphosis

Feel your kinship with the wind
take on a new energy, a collaboration of souls,
whispers of shifting currents.

Feel your kinship with fire
take on a new energy, an external spark
keeping company with your inner flame.

Feel your kinship with the water
take on a new energy, a pull from deep within,
a call older than time.

Feel your kinship with the land
take on a new energy, a pull from your foundation,
ancient bedrock's song of solace.

Allow your feet to become deep roots
thirsty for earth's elixir, your legs stems
of a mighty oak, spine straight and true as a sequoia.

Reaching arms of spring seedlings
around the sun, bloom like summer
as silken locks of autumn milkweed dance with a winter sky.

With eyes of Raven and ears of Fox, taste
each day with Hummingbird's tongue, always seeking
earth's sweet nectar, each season's hymn of light.

Then the time comes to lay your body
down in the water, a returning to earth,
heart finding home in the clouds

to dream in a language known
by osprey and otter, pine tree and pebble,
mist rising through the moors, claiming you

as one of the wild.

Enough of this world
after Teddy Macker

You can never have enough
of this world,
and that's part
of the mystery, isn't it?

Instead, all we can do
is see red flowers
as they drop their petals
each one a crimson offering
a delicate gift given just once,
each one, and then they're gone.

Instead, all we can do
is feel how sun and wind and rain
all have their own language of touch
each one a burst of tactile energy
an elemental shift given
day after day, season after season
always repeating, never the same.

Instead, all we can do
is notice the nuance
pervading all of life
each detail another thread weaving
a continual stitching (and mending where necessary)
of earth's collective tapestry.

Instead, all we can do
is wonder at how praising
things that cannot last
holds the world for us, somehow
allowing what we do have
of this world to be enough.

River, amen

Let's go down
to the river to pray,

whatever praying
means to you—

ingesting beauty
listening to stones
finding songs in your pockets.

Fill your heart with the harmonies
that pull beneath the surface.

Allow whatever prayer
finds you to be enough.

AFTERWORD

The move from autumn to winter, or summer to fall, or winter to spring, any transitional time really, is usually blustery where I live in Minnesota. One November not so many years ago, snow fell every day for a week. Then the sun came out again, but the cold winds gusted, leaving the lake behind the house unsettled and ringed with just a bit of ice around the edge. The morning of the returning sunshine, I woke to find 20 trumpeter swans in the open water. Earlier that week there had been two, then a few more came, and finally they claimed the little body of water as their place, at least for a time. Then I saw a juvenile heron, looking none too pleased with the cold temperature, head tucked in and feathers plumped as she stood in the shallows. A hawk cried overhead, and the pileated woodpecker drummed in the distance. Sandhill cranes trilled, great wings flapping in time with the geese on their way south. A downy woodpecker pecked at the suet cake hanging off the back deck, and three chickadees hopped up the trunk of one of the basswoods.

I like to think of these birds, the ones that are always present as well as those only here for a while each year as they migrate through, as my neighbors, along with the other life forms who share this land. Kin, even, since we earth dwellers are all connected by the simple fact that we rely on this shared planet to keep our bodies alive. Sister swans. Wood duck brothers. Uncle owl, grandfather maple, auntie ermines. The otters teach us to play and the coyote reminds us to use our voices. When my daughter was in fourth grade, she kept some stink bugs in a terrarium along with some moss and lichen as companions. Bug babies with a mossy nanny. Grandfather maple lost a limb that year, and he gifted it to us as firewood. A few deer give their lives each autumn to become part of our sustenance. Plants that thrive in the garden become compost to nourish next year's seedlings.

We're all a part of the whole, and we're all just wild enough—which is something to remember and hold close. We are part of the elements that make up the holy wild and mysteriously wonderful body of earth. We are wind, fire, water, and earth, meeting in space and across time with amens in all languages weaving us together.

Notes

The East, South, West, North, Center framework was inspired by the invocation gifted to me by Christina Beck for a retreat series called The Art of Living Wild.

The poem titled "The young ones" was first published under the title "To Be On Earth" in *Woodland Manitou* (2017).

The poems titled "Life on Earth" and "Thin Places" appeared in ArtReach St. Croix's Poets of Place chapbook (2022).

The poems titled "Passion" and "Oneness" were first published in *Cold Spring Hallelujah* (2019).

The poems "On Certainty" and "On Uncertainty" were first published as a duo in Micro Lit Almanac (APRIL 2022).

The poem "Necessary undoing" was inspired by a poem called "Darkness, be my undoing" by Krissy Kludt.

"Enough of this world" was inspired by Teddy Macker's poem in his collection, *This World* thanks to a prompt from **Writing the Wild**, a year long writing course.

The final poem's title, "River, amen" is also the title of Michael Garrigan's second poetry collection.

ACKNOWLEDGMENTS

Thank you to my family, especially Nick and Eva, for always being there.

Thank you to Connor Wolfe, for believing in my work and helping me bring it to life.

Thank you to Barbara Brown, for allowing Cedar Intimacy to grace the cover of this collection, and for years of support via sharing my work on social media.

Thank you to Amy Carrier, for your enthusiastic support and regular readings of my poetry at your wilderness and wellness events.

Thank you to Krissy Kludt and *Writing the Wild*, for providing such a beautiful creative container as I finished this manuscript.

Thank you to Eric Lehman and Frank Inzan Owen, for your early offers to review and give feedback on this collection.

Thank you to all who pick this book up and spend time with these words. Your attention is a gift.

About the Cover Artist

Barbara Brown's intimacy with the woods is reflected in her paintings. She captures the enchantment of the forest with her juxtaposition of realism lovingly rendered, with otherworldly symbolism and/or geometric elements—sometimes hidden, always spellbinding. Barbara holds a Bachelor of Science in Geography and a Diploma of Fine Art. She lives in the wild, forested mountains of the Slocan Valley in the remote West Kootenay region of southeastern British Columbia, Canada, with her husband and a cat or two. As an award winning painter, she shows her work annually in the Columbia Basin Culture Tour as well as online via Manhattan Arts International. Learn more about her work at barbarabrownart.com.

About the Cover Painting
In the Artist's Words

Cedar Intimacy
(Oil on Canvas, 18" x 14", Barbara Brown)

This image captivated me in the forest. First, up close and personal, I fell in love with the pretty surface patterns that those intense green twinkling cedar frond fingers make as they reach for the sun at the edge of a clearing on the mountainside.

Playful with its offering of beauty, she revels in her aliveness. Then ...I am invited to travel deeper; to delve into the dark forest beyond the surface, and there to be welcomed into the inner sanctum depths with, again, a twinkle of sunshine.

And, as happens so often in my work, the oval comes to me, with its soft feminine welcoming geometry to help me to convey the feeling inherent in this offering.

These are Western Red Cedar *(Thuja plicata)* which can grow to 130 feet tall and live for 1,000 years in the Inland Temperate Rainforest.

Cedar helps us to heal emotional hurts, and it is symbolic of the pure, the sublime, and the sacred.

About the Author

Heidi Barr is a writer and wellness coach whose work is founded on a commitment to cultivating ways of being that are life-giving and sustainable for people, communities, and the planet. She is the author of several books of creative nonfiction, including *Collisions of Earth and Sky* and *Woodland Manitou*, and co author of *12 Tiny things*. She's also authored two other poetry collections, one cookbook, and is editor of "The Mindful Kitchen," a wellness column in *The Wayfarer Magazine*. One of the inaugural Poets of Place for the lower St. Croix Valley, her poetry has been featured in numerous publications, including the *St. Paul Almanac* and *South Dakota in Poems*. She lives with her family in rural Minnesota, where they tend a large vegetable garden, explore nature, and do their best to live simply.

Learn more at heidibarr.com.

homebound
PUBLICATIONS

Homebound Publications is a Trans/Queer Owned publishing house based in the Berkshire Mountains. What began during a brainstorming session in a Boston cafe has become a platform for hundreds of indie authors. More than a company, we are a community of writers and readers exploring the larger questions we face as a global village. We publish full-length works of creative non-fiction and poetry.

homeboundpublications.com

WAYFARER

BASED IN THE BERKSHIRE MOUNTAINS, MASS.

At Wayfarer Books we believe poetry is the language of the earth. We believe words—shaped like rivers through wild places—can change the shape of the world. We publish poets and writers and renegades who stand outside of mainstream culture—poets, essayists, and storytellers whose work might withstand the scrutiny of crows and coyotes, those who are cryptic and floral, the crepuscular, and the queer-at-heart. We are more than just a publisher but a community of writers. Our mission is to produce books that can serve as a compass and map to all wayfarers through wild terrain.

WAYFARERBOOKS.ORG

www.ingramcontent.com/pod-product-compliance
Lightning Source LLC
Chambersburg PA
CBHW031421120626
46545CB00006B/2211